JOURNAL

PETER PAUPER PRESS, INC.
WHITE PLAINS, NEW YORK

PETER PAUPER PRESS
Fine Books and Gifts Since 1928

Our Company

In 1928, at the age of twenty-two, Peter Beilenson began printing books on a small press in the basement of his parents' home in Larchmont, New York. Peter—and later, his wife, Edna—sought to create fine books that sold at "prices even a pauper could afford."

Today, still family owned and operated, Peter Pauper Press continues to honor our founders' legacy—and our customers' expectations—of beauty, quality, and value.

Images used under license from Shutterstock.com
Designed by Tesslyn Pandarakalam

Visit us at www.peterpauper.com

The bannana

there wons was
a family they
where so exited
because they where
going on a CRUIS!
they where sooo
exited. The Next
day time to go!!
let's go guys said
the dad oK
said the kids. When
they got there
they where about
to get on the
boat honk here
comes the boar
time to go..
on are you
guys ready
to get on

let's go so
they went on
half way in the
ride one of there
kids said hey
mom I think the
enigine is running
out of battary
O NO!! It is
and look we are
headed straight for
that island O NO
they all said agran
WOOSh! The
Next thing they
New they where
on an island
since we are
here let's go see
if we can.
find some

food OK they
all said so they
whent to go
see what typ's
of food there
is o look there
is a bannana tree
one of the
family members climad
up the tree
he said hey guys
what they replied
you whant belive
what I just found
what did you find?
you wont belive
me I found
a talking bannana
what!!!! the
family asked what
is your name?

My name is
bannana joe
Hi there Joe bannana
joe hi he
said I will
show you all
the best spots
on the island
OK they said.
So they whent
whith him Lets
go said bannana
Joe they followed
him this is
taking for ever.
your right said
the children we
are here said
bannana Joe
wogoo!!! they
said it's a
water fall

We can walk in bannana Joe said let's go they said.

UwU

UwU

Uи

MOM

Team

For life

:)

Bunngys adven

Once upon a time there
was a little bunny called
bunngy and and bunggys
friend jack. They were
animals waiting to get
adopded. and there was a
animal called shadow because
he was always in shadows.
But then One day late late
at night shadow escaped and
after that no one was safe
excNt old old master loo
he is the only one who is
safe because of shadow,
everything but one little tinee
flower saved the day but
other days i'm not sher he
could come back he could.

1

chapter 1

The flower blue away now none of us know what to do. But then at the second another flower came it was like it was calling our name. But the flower was strange it looked I don't know all I know was it wasn't the same. Then Shadow showed up a little like the flower weird but over powered. Then something happened Shadow shrank the size of a little butterfly and ran away like a cheeta. But then some thing happened he turned biger and biger and big er and biger like a giant. But then he came back it was strange but we made it work. He rumbled and grumbled. But then he was gone. It took us a longtime to beliesed he won't come back then I cryed

because I missed him for
some reason I don't know
why but I felt sad I'd never
see him again. Shadow was
gone I was sad really
really sad but what
made me even more sad
is everyone cheered loudly.
So what I did was big
oh it was big. I built a
spaceship but not just a
ordenary spaceship it was
better it was one to fly
high but when I looked
at it didn't look right
it needed glitter a lot of
glitter. I sparkled there
here and how you say
I prackdised every day.
It turned night time and
I tested the spaceship it
was fine but wasn't destised.

So I desided to make
it look like a car It
didn't look like a car
but it was a start but
for now it was good but
tomorow it should.